GIANT ANIMALS

SALTWATER CROCODILES

Susan Schafer

New York

Published in 2015 by Cavendish Square Publishing, LLC
243 5th Avenue, Suite 136, New York, NY 10016

Copyright © 2015 by Cavendish Square Publishing, LLC

First Edition

No part of this publication may be reproduced, stored in a retrieval system, or transmitted in any form or by any means—electronic, mechanical, photocopying, recording, or otherwise—without the prior permission of the copyright owner. Request for permission should be addressed to Permissions, Cavendish Square Publishing, 243 5th Avenue, Suite 136, New York, NY 10016. Tel (877) 980-4450; fax (877) 980-4454.

Website: cavendishsq.com

This publication represents the opinions and views of the author based on his or her personal experience, knowledge, and research. The information in this book serves as a general guide only. The author and publisher have used their best efforts in preparing this book and disclaim liability rising directly or indirectly from the use and application of this book.

CPSIA Compliance Information: Batch #WS14CSQ

All websites were available and accurate when this book was sent to press.

Library of Congress Cataloging-in-Publication Data
Schafer, Susan, author.
Saltwater crocodiles / Susan Schafer.
pages cm. — (Giant animals)
Includes index.
ISBN 978-1-62712-957-2 (hardcover) ISBN 978-1-62712-959-6 (ebook)
1. Crocodylus porosus—Juvenile literature. 2. Crocodiles—Juvenile literature. I. Title.

QL666.C925S336 2015
597.98'2—dc23

2014003916

Editorial Director: Dean Miller
Editor: Andrew Coddington
Copy Editor: Cynthia Roby
Art Director: Jeffrey Talbot
Designer: Joseph Macri
Photo Researcher: J8 Media
Production Manager: Jennifer Ryder-Talbot
Production Editor: David McNamara

The photographs in this book are used by permission and through the courtesy of: Cover photo by Mchugh Tom/Photo Researchers/Getty Images; © The Natural History Museum / The Image Works, 4; Smokeybjb/File:Pakasuchus.jpg/Wikimedia Commons, 8; Joseph Macri for Cavendish Square, 10; SShukla/File:Marsh crocodile or Magar at Ranganathittu Sanctuary (pix SShukla).JPG/Wikipedia, 13; Denise Thompson/Shutterstock.com, 13; © Lacz, Gerard / Animals Animals – All rights reserved, 14; © Photoshot, 16; © ecopic, 17; Jeff Rotman/Photonica/Getty Images, 18; Digital Vision/Thinkstock, 19; John Hay/Lonely Planet Images/Getty Images, 20; samuraioasis/Shutterstock.com, 21; Reinhard Dirscherl/Visuals Unlimited, Inc./Getty Images, 23; Paul Chesley/National Geographic/Getty Images, 24; Rasmussen AR, Murphy JC, Ompi M, Gibbons JW, Uetz P (2011)/File:Distribution of the saltwater crocodile, Crocodylus porosus - journal.pone.0027373.g004.png/Wikimedia Commons, 26; Raúl Barrero photography/Flickr/Getty Images, 27; Jonathan and Angela Scott/The Image Bank/Getty Images, 29; ©Ben & Lynn Cropp/Auscape/The Image Works, 30; Sadi Ugur OKa!u/E+/Getty Images, 32; Gallo Images-Roger De La Harpe/The Image Bank/Getty Images, 33; Eye Ubiquitous / SuperStock, 34; Mattstone911/File:American Crocodile in Jamaica.jpg/Wikimedia Commons, 37; Tyrone Turner/National Geographic/Getty Images, 38; Richard I'Anson/Lonely Planet Images/Getty Images, 40; Rex Features via AP Images, 43.

Printed in the United States of America

CONTENTS

Chapter One   Out of the Age of Reptiles   **5**

Chapter Two   Primitive, But Not Simple   **15**

Chapter Three   Beach Bums   **25**

Chapter Four   Hurt by Its Reputation   **35**

Glossary   **44**

Find Out More   **46**

Index   **47**

About the Author   **48**

OUT OF THE AGE OF REPTILES

A crocodile moves slowly and silently forward, peering intently at a small animal just ahead. Its powerful tail trails behind. With a sudden lunge forward and a snap of its muscular jaws, it grabs its **prey** between sharp, protruding teeth. It is the ultimate **predator**, like a shark in the sea, but this crocodile is not in the water. It is hunting on land.

The time is nearly 200 million years ago during the early Jurassic period of Earth. The first crocodiles are running with the dinosaurs. Measuring only about 3 feet (1 meter) long, they are miniatures compared to today's largest living crocodile, the saltwater crocodile. The saltwater crocodile reaches lengths of up to 23 feet (7 m) and can weigh in at more than 2,200 pounds (1,000 kilograms).

First Crocodile

One of the earliest fossils of a crocodile, the miniature crocodile has been named *Protosuchus*. *Protosuchus* literally means "first crocodile" in Greek. It was the first in the ancestral line that would eventually give rise to the saltwater crocodile, and it had many characteristics in common with modern crocodiles.

Many of the bones that formed this first crocodile's skull are shared by modern crocodiles. Its snout was broad at the base, which allowed for more muscles to attach to the bone. This gave it a stronger, snapping bite. It had protective body armor in the form of tough outer scales and bony **scutes** within the skin, just like crocodiles today. It had lower teeth that fit into notches on either side of the upper jaw. When its mouth was closed, the teeth stuck out, giving it the same snaggletoothed look of a modern crocodile.

Unlike the saltwater crocodile, however, *Protosuchus* was not aquatic—meaning it did not live in the water. Its legs, particularly its hind legs, were longer for running on land. Its eyes were positioned more on the sides of its skull, which was an adaptation for terrestrial life and being able to see both in front of and behind them. (Modern crocodiles have eyes on the top of their skull, which allows them to see while floating in the water.) In spite of the differences, scientists agree that *Protosuchus* represents the first of the crocodiles to appear on Earth.

Rise of the Ruling Lizards

Protosuchus descended from a group of reptiles called the archosaurs, which literally means "ruling lizards." Archosaurs were lizard-like—probably insect-eating animals—that dominated Earth after the largest extinction event ever, which occurred in the Permian Period more than 250 million years ago. Called the "Great Dying," the mass extinction killed around 96 percent of all of the species living at the time. Scientists don't know what caused the Great Dying, but some of the **hypotheses** include enormous volcanic explosions, methane gas polluting the air, acid rain, or an asteroid hitting Earth. All of life on Earth today is descended from the 4 percent of species that survived.

Before the Great Dying, a group of mammal-like reptiles called synapsids were the largest land animals. Scientists say that any animal at the time longer than 3 feet (1 m) was a synapsid. Only a few of the small synapsid species survived the extinction to eventually give rise to mammals. The archosaurs, however, were able to recolonize the newly opened land, giving rise to an abundance of animals of all shapes and sizes, from crocodiles to dinosaurs. For the next 170 million years—throughout the Mesozoic period—the archosaurs ruled Earth. Because of this, the Mesozoic is often called the Age of Reptiles.

Back to the Sea

During the Age of Reptiles, the archosaurs formed two major branches. One branch produced the crocodiles, led by *Protosuchus*. Another branch created the dinosaurs, pterosaurs, and eventually birds. Most people are surprised to learn that crocodiles are actually more closely related to dinosaurs and birds than they are to lizards, whose ancestors rose from a different line.

Because crocodiles descended from a terrestrial—or land-based—ancestor, they are called "secondarily aquatic." That means the saltwater crocodile came from a line of aquatic, ocean-dwelling ancestors (before the archosaurs) that adapted to terrestrial life on land and finally returned to an aquatic life. The saltwater crocodile, then, has come full circle and returned to the oceans of its ancestors, where it is often found along shorelines and even in the sea.

Cat Crocodile

A hundred million years ago when crocodiles were widespread and diverse, one unusual species of crocodile lived in what is now Tanzania in southeast Africa. It had the characteristics of a crocodile, including the protruding canine teeth of the saltwater crocodile, but it also had the mammal-like characteristics of a cat. Named *Pakasuchus*, it was about the size of a pet cat with long, slender legs and a flexible backbone for moving swiftly on land. Its name comes from the Swahili word *paka*, which means "cat," and the Greek word *suchus*, for crocodile.

Because *Pakasuchus* was active, scientists believe it was probably endothermic, or warm-blooded. Like the cat (and unlike the crocodile), it had a flexible jaw and grinding molars with shearing edges that allowed it to chew its food. Before the discovery of ancient crocodiles such as the cat crocodile, scientists believed that shearing teeth and endothermy were unique only to **carnivorous** mammals.

From Warm to Cold

Because terrestrial animals were active, many scientists now believe that the early archosaurs were endothermic, or warm-blooded. This means that these animals generated their own internal heat to keep their bodies warm. Birds, which came from the same early ancestry as the crocodiles, are also endothermic. Modern crocodiles such as the saltwater crocodile are ectothermic—or cold-blooded—which means that their body temperature varies with the environment. They cannot generate their own internal heat.

Using the term cold-blooded to describe a crocodile, however, is misleading because crocodiles are rarely cold. The body temperature of a saltwater crocodile, for example, is maintained year round between about 80 and 89 degrees Fahrenheit (27 and 32 degrees Celsius), depending on the **habitat** and the season of the year. Ectothermic animals maintain their body temperature behaviorally by moving in and out of the sun. At the same time, if their heat source is not available, their metabolism slows and they can tolerate lower temperatures than normal. The fact that some ancient crocodiles were endothermic and became secondarily ectothermic is probably what saved them during another major extinction event that occurred at the end of the Mesozoic period.

During the mid to late Mesozoic period, between 200 and sixty-five million years ago, crocodiles had diversified into hundreds of different kinds of crocodiles that lived in all types of habitats from terrestrial to aquatic. Terrestrial crocodiles remained land-based, and aquatic crocodiles became ectothermic. Then a massive asteroid hit Earth around sixty-five million years ago at the end of the Mesozoic period. Scientists believe the explosion resulted, at least in part, in the second greatest extinction of all time after the Great Dying. Nearly 50 percent of the world's species were lost, including all of the dinosaurs. The aquatic species of crocodiles, however, survived. Because they were ectothermic, they were able to tolerate the lower temperatures that resulted when the debris from the impact of the asteroid blocked the sun's warmth.

Giants Lost

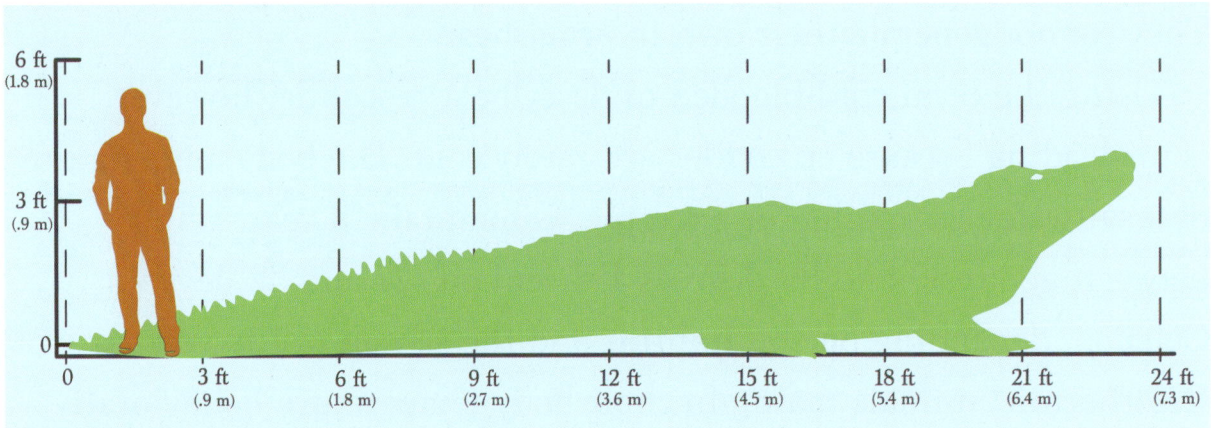

An adult human is dwarfed when compared to the size of a saltwater crocodile.

At its maximum length of 23 feet (7 m), the saltwater crocodile holds the record for the largest living crocodile. It is not, however, the largest crocodile that ever existed. Near the end of the Mesozoic period, *Deinosuchus* patrolled the **estuarine** waters along the coast of what is now North America. Scientists now believe that *Deinosuchus*, which means "terrible crocodile," was more closely related to early alligators that branched off from the crocodile line. Either way, it grew to a whopping 50 feet (15 m) in length—that's longer than three passenger cars set end-to-end!

The largest known true crocodile—one closely related to the saltwater crocodile—was discovered in fossil beds in what is now Africa. It was named *Crocodylus thorbjarnarsoni*, or Thorbjarnarsoni's crocodile, after a famous crocodile expert. It grew to a length of 27 feet (8.3 m), not much more than the saltwater crocodile, and lived a mere two million years ago.

Survivors of the Dinosaur Age

Crocodilians and birds are the only archosaurs that survive today. The only reptiles that have been around longer are the turtles and the tuataras, which are unusual lizard-like reptiles that live only in New Zealand. Crocodilians belong to the order *Crocodylia*, a group of reptiles (class *Reptilia*) that includes crocodiles, alligators, caimans, and gavials. Three closely related families of crocodilians are recognized within the order: *Crocodylidae*, *Alligatoridae*, and *Gavialidae*.

The saltwater crocodile belongs to the crocodile family: the family *Crocodylidae*. Its scientific name is *Crocodylus porosus*. *Crocodylus* comes from the combined Greek words, *kroko* and *deilos*, and means "pebble worm." The species name *porosus* has both Greek and Latin roots, and means "having many calluses." A callus is a thickened, hardened part of the skin. The name refers to the crocodile's bumpy skin.

The saltwater crocodile is also called the estuarine crocodile or, in Australia, simply "saltie." It is not only the largest living crocodile, but also the largest living reptile and the largest **riparian**, or river-based, predator. Flatten a T-Rex so it crawls and swims, and you have a saltwater crocodile.

Most surviving crocodilian species are crocodiles. Of the twenty-three living species, fourteen belong to the crocodile family.

The family *Alligatoridae* includes the alligators and their smaller relatives, the caimans. A four-legged reptile, caimans closely resemble alligators but measure only about 4 to 6 feet (1.2 to 1.8 m) in length. The family *Gavialidae* includes a single species, the gavial (or gharial). The gavial is a large, fish-eating crocodilian with an extremely narrow snout. It is found only on the Indian subcontinent, a southerly region of Asia.

Crocodilians have changed little over time and because they all look similar on the outside, it can be difficult to tell them apart unless you are familiar with them. Most people think that alligators have a wide, rounded snout, while crocodiles have a long, narrow snout. That might be generally true, but there are many exceptions. For example, the Indian mugger crocodile has a wide snout, and some New World caimans have narrow snouts. The gavial has the narrowest snout of all, but it is neither an alligator nor a crocodile. Exploring the animals' skeletal structures is the best way to tell crocodilians apart.

One characteristic that can be seen on the outside distinguishes crocodiles from alligators—if you care to get close enough to see it. The fourth lower tooth on the lower jaw of a crocodile fits into a notch in the upper jaw, making the tooth visible when the mouth is closed. In an alligator, the fourth lower tooth fits into a socket in the upper jaw, so the tooth disappears when the alligator's mouth is closed.

The fourth tooth in the lower jaw of a crocodile (top) fits into a notch in the upper jaw so it shows on the outside when the mouth is closed. In the alligator (bottom), this tooth fits in a socket and is hidden.

PRIMITIVE, BUT NOT SIMPLE

The saltwater crocodile is a survivor. Its relatives have lived for millions of years through climate changes, mass extinctions, and competition with other animals—yet it looks much the same as crocodiles always have. For this reason, many people say that crocodiles look **primitive**.

The saltwater crocodile may look prehistoric, but it is anything but simple. Like other crocodiles, it is an intelligent and fierce predator, yet the females are gentle parents. In many ways it is as advanced as its relatives, the birds. It builds a nest, and its jaws and teeth are specialized for grabbing prey. It also has keen senses and special glands to help it live in salty water. The saltwater crocodile has one of the most complex hearts of all **vertebrates**—it has four chambers (the same as the human heart), and its beat can be slowed to one per every thirty seconds or so. It is a strong swimmer with nose and ear valves, specialized lungs, and excellent navigation skills.

Armed to the Teeth

The saltwater crocodile is a carnivorous eating machine. Its mouth is large enough to toss back and swallow such large animals as wallabies, monkeys, or sharks, in one gulp. It can't chew, however. If its food is too large to swallow, such as a cow or buffalo, it clamps down on it and rolls, twisting off a smaller piece. Sometimes more than one crocodile will grab the same prey, ripping it apart. A saltwater crocodile can eat up to half of its weight in one meal, but it can also go for months without eating anything at all.

When a saltwater crocodile feeds, it grabs its prey and throws it back into its throat without chewing.

The saltwater crocodile has a heavy jaw, which helps it to withstand the forces involved in biting and tearing its food. The jaw muscles are extremely strong, generating up to 5,000 pounds of pressure per square inch. In contrast, humans can only clamp down with about 100 pounds of pressure per square inch! If the saltwater crocodile loses teeth when feeding, new ones grow in quickly. Over its lifetime, a saltwater crocodile might go through thousands of teeth.

Although saltwater crocodiles are gruesome feeders, attacks on humans are rare, and in most of those cases people put themselves in harm's way. Even as a large adult, a saltwater crocodile normally feeds on small animals, such as fish, crabs, turtles, birds, rats, and monkeys. That doesn't mean they won't take whatever they can overpower, including pigs, wallabies, cattle, sharks, and even other crocodiles. Younger saltwater crocodiles that measure up to about 6 feet (2 m) long feed on smaller prey, such as insects, small fish, frogs, and shrimp.

When hunting, a saltwater crocodile glides toward its prey with only its eyes and nose exposed. Its rough, olive-brown or black **mottled** skin helps it blend with the water like a floating log. The body of older adults is often covered with algae, making it even harder to see.

A saltwater crocodile might also lurk under the water, waiting for prey to pass. It can hold its breath for up to three hours. Special organs in the saltwater crocodile's skin act as motion sensors to help it detect

Looking like a log floating in the water, a saltwater crocodile sneaks up on its prey.

when anything is near. These pimple-like sensors are particularly handy when hunting at night or in muddy water because the crocodile doesn't need to see its prey. Instead, the crocodile can feel it moving nearby.

Often, a saltwater crocodile learns where animals come to drink and will wait for one to reach the edge of the water. When it sees its chance, it lunges forward and drags the prey under the water to drown.

The saltwater crocodile is also a scavenger. Using its keen sense of smell, it might travel for miles (kilometers) to find the stinking **carcass** of a dead animal. Although it usually hunts at night, it will eat whenever and wherever it can.

A Suit of Armor

A saltwater crocodile's skin is made of thick scales that do not overlap. Under the scales of the neck and back are flat pieces of bone called osteoderms. Together with scales, the osteoderms form tough, ridged plates or scutes, which provide the saltwater crocodile its own built-in suit of armor.

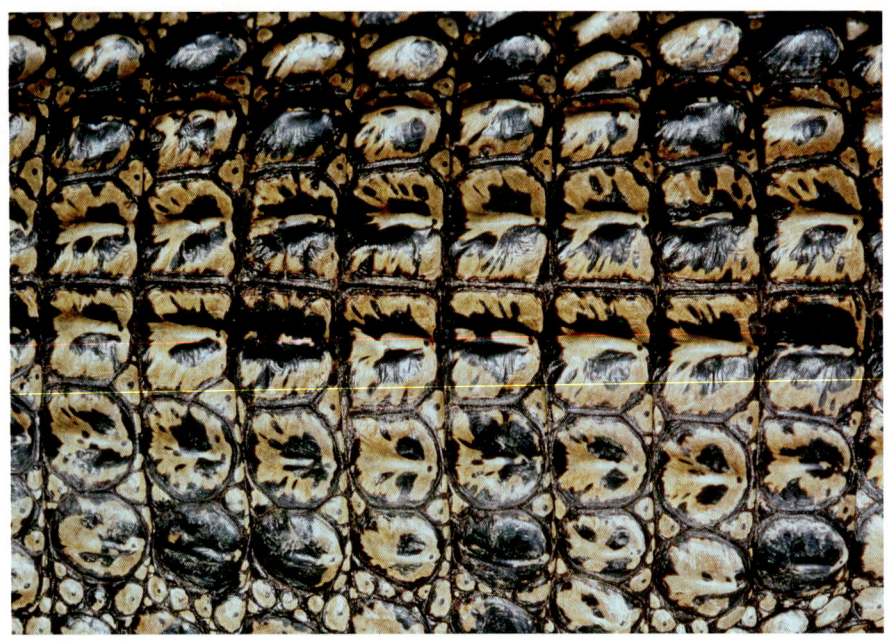

The skin of a saltwater crocodile shows the tough scutes that protect it like armor.

The scutes also act as heating and cooling plates, which help the crocodile control its body temperature. Because the scutes form a pattern unique to each type of crocodile, scientists can use them to tell the different species apart. Scutes are found in all crocodilians, but have also been found in the remains of some dinosaurs, such as Stegosaurus, and in some lizards, such as the Gila monster. They are even found in a few mammals, such as the armadillo.

Safety Valves

The saltwater crocodile has a sensitive nose, sharp ears, and keen eyes. Just like humans, its nose has two external openings, or nostrils. The nostrils are on the top of the end of its long nose. When it wants to breathe without being seen, a crocodile sticks only its nostrils out of the water.

When a saltwater crocodile dives, muscular valves over the nostrils snap shut to seal out water. Muscular flaps also clamp down over the ears. Some people put on nose and earplugs while swimming, but a crocodile is already wearing them.

A saltwater crocodile's eyes have elliptical pupils that are narrow, like a cat's, rather than round like a human's. This shape allows better night vision. A crocodile can open and close its eyelids, but it also has a third eyelid that is clear and slides sideways across each eye. The third eyelid acts as a pair of swimming goggles, allowing the crocodile to see underwater while protecting the eyes from damage.

The pupil of a crocodile's eye is narrow like a cat's, which helps it see better at night.

Out to Sea

The saltwater crocodile can swim like an Olympian. To swim, the saltwater crocodile pushes its strong, muscular tail from side to side. It is such a strong swimmer that it is not unusual to find one hundreds of miles (kilometers) out to sea. Its webbed feet, however, are not used for swimming, but for making quick, sharp turns.

A saltwater crocodile propels itself through the water by pushing its strong, muscular tail from side to side.

A saltwater crocodile can swim up to 20 miles (32 km) per hour, although normally it would cruise at a much slower speed. Scientists have attached transmitters to a number of individuals and discovered that they can travel for days at a time, covering hundreds of miles in just a few weeks. In fact, scientists tracked one 12.6-foot (3.8-meter) male saltie who left Australia's Kennedy River and traveled 366 miles (590 km) over twenty-five days. The reasons for the salties' journeys—which are common—are unknown to scientists.

The large tongue of the saltwater crocodile is used to cool off its body, get rid of excess salt, and carry its young.

The saltwater crocodile lives in both freshwater and saltwater environments. Living in salty water, however, has its challenges. The crocodile has to get rid of excess salt that enters its body when it swallows its food. To do this, it has specialized salt glands on its tongue. Any extra salt in its body is **excreted** through these glands and washed back into the water. Alligators don't have the same glands because they live only in freshwater environments.

Advanced Lungs and Heart

Like other mammals, when humans breathe, the air flows into their lungs through branched airways, called **bronchi**, that get progressively smaller. The bronchi eventually end in small sacs called **alveoli**. In the alveoli, the oxygen moves from the air into the bloodstream to be taken to the body cells. At the same time, carbon dioxide moves from the bloodstream into the alveoli to be exhaled. When the air moves into the lungs, it goes back out the same way it came in.

A saltwater crocodile, however, does not have alveoli. It has lungs with one-way airflow like a bird's, which supports the idea that they shared a common ancestor. Scientists first believed that only birds had one-way air flow as an adaptation to support the high oxygen demands of flight. Now that the same system has been found in crocodiles, scientists believe the lungs must have developed in archosaurs before the crocodilians branched off from the line that led to dinosaurs and birds.

When a saltwater crocodile inhales, air flows through its windpipe and into the first two branches of the bronchi, which lead into the lungs. But when the bronchi branches for the second time, one branch takes a sharp turn away from the main direction of the airflow, creating what is called an aerodynamic valve. Air rushes past the valve, carrying oxygen to the cells of the body and eventually returning in a one-way loop. The system is highly efficient, allowing the saltwater crocodile to stay underwater for long periods.

The saltwater crocodile's heart helps it stay under the water for even longer periods of time. Like modern birds and mammals, it has a heart with four chambers. However, it is even more advanced than birds and mammals because it has two **aortas** for oxygen-rich blood to flow through with a **shunt** between them. The shunt allows the blood carrying the most oxygen to be diverted to areas where it is most needed, such as the brain. At the same time, the blood with the least amount of oxygen goes where it is least needed, such as the legs and tail. Because the crocodile is resting while underwater, it doesn't need its legs and tail to move.

The saltwater crocodile has a specialized heart and lungs to help it stay under water for hours.

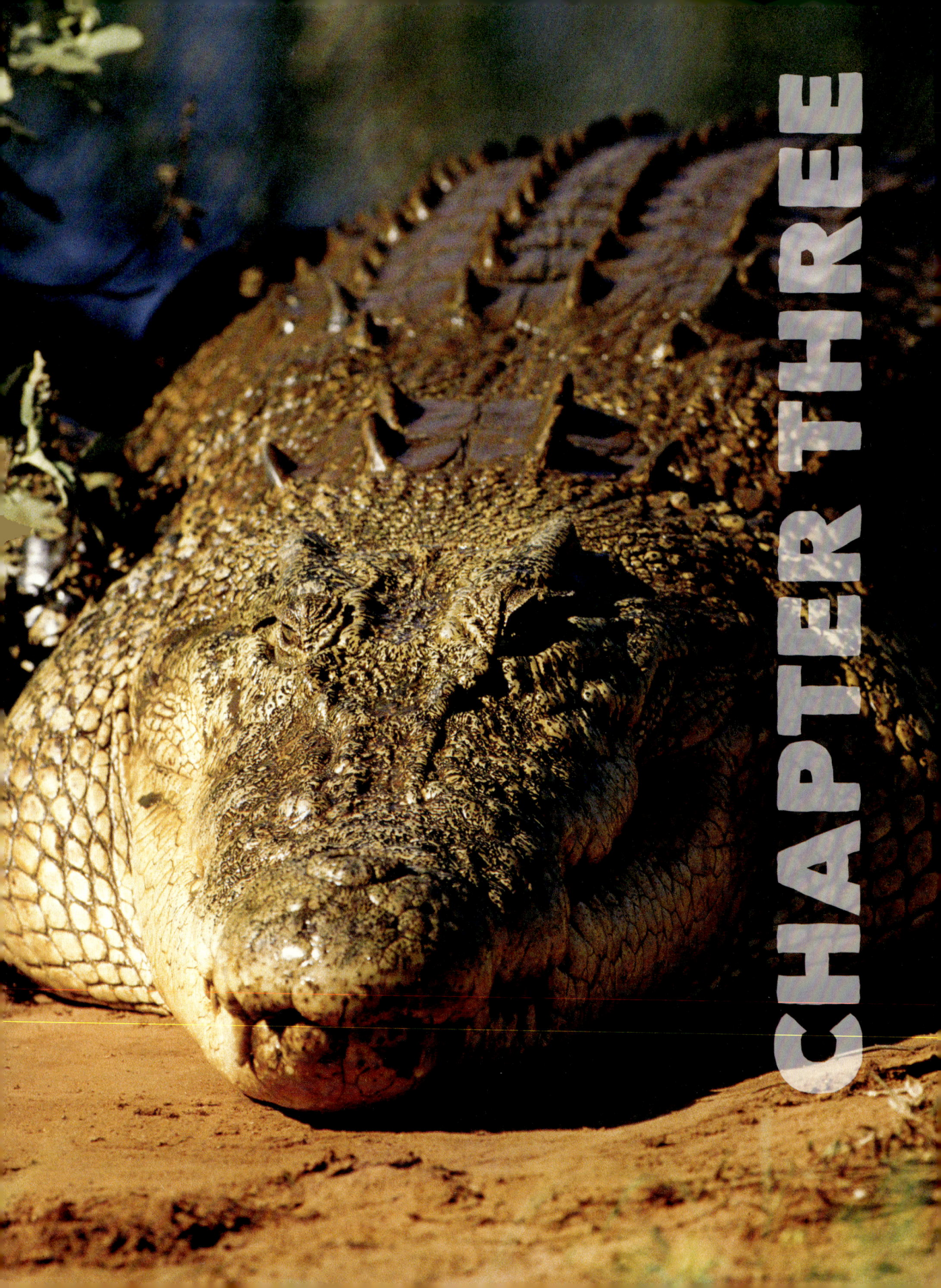

CHAPTER THREE

BEACH BUMS

Imagine lying on a tropical beach all day, sometimes diving into the water to cool off. You leave the beach only in search of food. That pretty much describes a day in the life of a saltwater crocodile. It is often seen basking in the sun just out of the water, warming its large body.

Sometimes it lies with its mouth open, its heavy lower jaw lying on the ground and the entire top of its head tilted upward. It has no sweat glands, so if it gets too hot, it gapes its mouth to release heat through evaporation. It may even plunge into the water to cool off.

Going Tropical

The saltwater crocodile ranges across a wider area than any of the other crocodiles. It is found in warm, wet tropical areas from eastern India and Sri Lanka, throughout Southeast Asia and the Philippines, and south through Indonesia and Papua New Guinea to northern Australia. In spite of its name, it is found in freshwater rivers, inland lakes, swamps, and marshes, as well as in coastal lagoons and estuaries. Estuaries are found at the mouths of rivers where their freshwater mixes with the saltwater from the sea.

Because it is a strong swimmer, the saltwater crocodile is also found on a number of offshore islands, such as those along the Great Barrier Reef of Australia. Some have even arrived on the Cocos (Keeling) Islands, located more than 600 miles (966 km) out to sea in the Indian Ocean northwest of Australia. These wayward individuals spend so much time out to sea that they sometimes have barnacles growing on their backs like many seafaring ships.

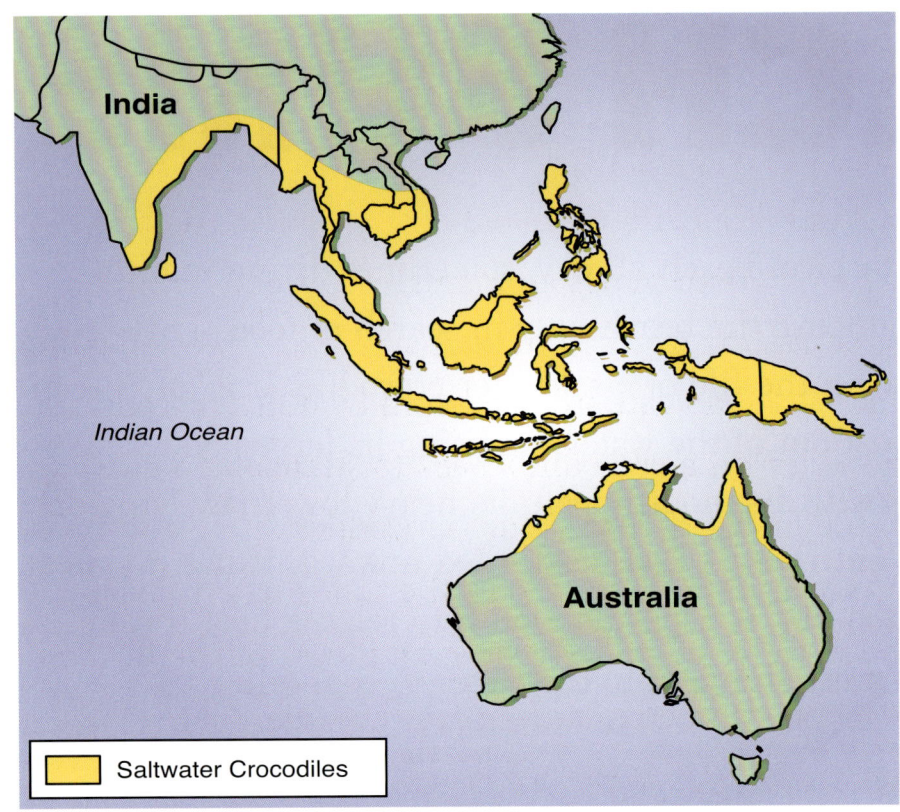

The saltwater crocodile is found over a wider range than any other crocodile.

Boss Croc

Male saltwater crocodiles set up territories where they rule over all others within that area. The larger the male, the more likely he will become the **dominant** male, known as the "boss croc." A boss croc has access to the best feeding areas and the best choice of mates, but he also provides stability to the area by keeping other crocodiles in line, preventing fights, and keeping out intruders. He has a calming effect on the territory's entire population.

In a stable population, the boss croc doesn't have to fight and risk injury to maintain peace. Instead, he "talks" to troublemakers and tries to convince them to behave or leave the area. Again, while saltwater crocodiles may look primitive, their sophisticated "language" proves them otherwise.

Talk to Me

The saltwater crocodile's language includes head slapping, nasal geysering, tail wagging, hissing, coughing, bubbling, grunting, growling, audible bellowing, sub-audible bellowing, and other sounds. Audible bellowing, which is used by both males and females to signal their location, is a sound that can be heard by humans. Sub-audible bellowing cannot be heard by humans and can only be heard by other crocodiles. The sound causes the water on a crocodile's back to sizzle and dance, sending vibrations through the water to other crocodiles.

Most of the communication takes place in the water when males signal their dominance to other males. For example, a saltwater crocodile head slaps by opening its mouth above the water and slapping it shut as it smacks down on top of the water, creating a big splash.

A boss crocodile uses a special "language" to keep other male crocodiles out of its territory, but it will attack if ignored.

During nasal geysering, the crocodile puts its nose just under the water and blows air out of its nostrils, causing two streams of water to spray upward into the air. Some of the signals, such as bellowing, nasal geysering, and tail wagging, are used in combination, presumably to change what a saltwater crocodile is trying to say. Scientists don't know exactly what they are saying, but the crocodiles do.

When out of the water, male and female saltwater crocodiles hiss when an intruder approaches. Females in particular hiss when they are defending their nests. To hiss, a saltwater crocodile opens its mouth and lets out a long, slow breath.

Water Dance

As the wet season approaches, the breeding season of the saltwater crocodile begins. During this time, the males become extremely aggressive, defending a larger territory than usual. One male may control a territory from two to five square miles (7 to 12 sq km). Just two square miles (7 sq km) covers about 500 city blocks in the midwestern United States.

Day and night, a boss croc spends his time chasing off other males. If an intruder won't leave, a battle may ensue. Biting and slamming their heavy head down on one another like sledgehammers, the two males fight until one gives up and swims away.

To attract a female, males bellow loudly. Females bellow in return. If a female likes a male, he courts her—rumbling softly, blowing bubbles, and gently rubbing her with his jaw. Circling her, he eventually pushes her under the water for mating. If a female is not attracted to a bellowing male, she will growl and then hide under the water or swim away.

Female saltwater crocodiles are ready to reproduce at around age twelve. By then, they have grown to about 7.5 feet (2.3 m) long. Males don't mature until they are almost 11 feet (3.4 m) long, and about sixteen or seventeen years old.

Male saltwater crocodiles may battle fiercely over females and territories.

A Nest on Stilts

During the breeding season, the female saltwater crocodile defends her chosen nesting area, chasing off other females. About a month after mating, she looks for a place close to water, such as along a riverbank, to build a nest. She searches for a moist, muddy place on the ground surrounded by lots of vegetation.

The female's choice of a nesting place is critical because the rivers often flood during the rainy season. All of the young in the eggs will drown if her nest floods. Flooding is the main cause of **embryo** death in saltwater crocodiles. During some years, every single nest within an area is destroyed, and no young hatch. However, the nest must remain moist or the eggs will dry out. This rarely happens, however, because the saltwater crocodile nests during a season when it rains almost every afternoon.

Once the female chooses a site, she builds a large mound of mud, grasses, and other fallen vegetation. The mound helps to hide the nest and protect it from predators, such as large lizards or **feral** pigs. For several weeks, the female works on the nest mound until it is several feet tall and many feet wide.

Finally, she scoops a bowl about 8 to 11 inches (20 to 30 centimeters) deep in the middle of the mound, lays her eggs, and covers them. Because the eggs are above ground level, the young are protected even if there is a little flooding. It's like a nest on stilts.

Female saltwater crocodiles build a large nest on the ground for their eggs and defend it against intruders.

A Natural Incubator

A saltwater crocodile can lay anywhere from twenty-five to ninety eggs. The average female, however, lays about fifty to sixty. Each egg is about 3 inches (8 cm) long, much larger than a chicken egg. Within the nest, the eggs are warmed as the rotting vegetation decomposes and gives off heat, creating a natural incubator.

The temperature in the nest is important not only for the proper development of the young, but it also determines the gender. A nest temperature of about 89 degrees Fahrenheit (32 degrees Celsius) produces mostly males. Temperatures higher or lower than that produce mostly females.

A Protective Mother

A female saltwater crocodile remains with her nest, guarding it throughout an incubation period of about eighty to ninety days. Sometimes she builds a den for herself in the bushes nearby. A female saltwater crocodile is particularly dangerous during this time because she will attack anything that disturbs her nest, including humans who happen to be walking in the area unaware that a nest is nearby.

When a female saltwater crocodile first lays an egg, it is hard like that of a chicken's. Near the end of incubation, the shell starts to crack. Some of the shell falls away, exposing a soft, leathery layer underneath, which makes it easier for the young to break out. On the end of the hatchling's nose is a sharp bump called an "egg tooth." A hatchling uses its egg tooth to slice its way out of the egg. Once the young hatches, the egg tooth falls off.

Even before the young hatch, they croak to their mother. The female grunts in reply. Attracted by the calls of her young, she goes to the nest and helps dig them out. If she finds a hatchling still inside of its egg, she gently picks it up and rolls it around in her mouth until the baby hatches. The young are fully developed and measure about a foot (30 cm) long when they hatch.

Once the hatchlings are free, the female gently picks them up in her mouth, creating a carrying pouch in her tongue. She takes them to the water and releases them for their first swim, but her duties do not end there. She stays with them for many weeks, protecting them from predators.

Crocodiles hatch from chicken-like eggs.

A female crocodile gently carries its newly-hatched young to water.

The female regularly calls to her young to keep them together in a safe group. If the young feel threatened, they let out a duck-like quack and the mother rushes to their defense. Sometimes they even ride on their mother's back.

Eventually, the young leave to explore new areas, where they may eventually set up a territory of their own. Saltwater crocodiles live at least fifty years in the wild, although some scientists suggest they may live up to 100 years.

CHAPTER FOUR

HURT BY ITS REPUTATION

The saltwater crocodile is a large, aggressive predator that may attack other animals, including humans, for many reasons. It may attack because it is hungry, defending its territory—or in the case of a female, to protect its nest. Because saltwater crocodiles may eat pets, such as dogs, they may attack the owner who is with them as well. This is why the saltwater crocodile has a bad reputation. The saltwater crocodile is just doing what comes naturally, but being dubbed a "man-eater" doesn't help when efforts are made to protect the species from extinction.

Attacks Uncommon

Although it is no consolation to the people and their families who have been affected by a saltwater crocodile attack, the truth is that such encounters don't happen very often. Although there are around 200,000 to 300,000 saltwater crocodiles in the wild, the Crocodile Specialist Group of the International Union for the Conservation of Nature (IUCN) estimates that only about twenty to thirty attacks on humans occur each year throughout the saltwater crocodile's range. Many such attacks do not result in fatalities. In fact, many more people die each year because they fall off a horse or get stung by a bee or wasp.

Most saltwater crocodiles involved in attacks on humans are at least 9 feet (2.7 m) long. Attacks usually happen to people who are swimming or wading in the water where crocodiles live, so they could have been avoided. There is some concern that attacks may increase because conservation efforts have resulted in a significant increase in the numbers of crocodile.

"Nuisance" crocodiles—those that regularly endanger people or their animals—are often killed. In some countries, however, the so-called nuisances are captured and sent to crocodile farms. At one time, they were relocated, but relocated crocodiles often return to their original territory.

Hanging On

The saltwater crocodile is extinct in Thailand and the Seychelles Islands off the east coast of Africa. In other parts of its range, it is difficult to determine how well the saltwater crocodile is doing because it is found on so many offshore islands. Overall, however, it is doing well, especially in Australia, Indonesia, and Papua New Guinea, where most individuals are found today.

The saltwater crocodile has not always done so well. Before it was recognized as an endangered species in the 1980s, it had nearly disappeared completely. Through the efforts of many people and countries, its numbers have slowly increased. Its status was lowered one step—from endangered to vulnerable—in the 1990s. Today, it has recovered enough to be categorized as a species of least concern, which is the lowest ranking given by the IUCN. The saltwater crocodile's comeback is considered by many to be a conservation success story.

Made in America

Four true crocodiles live in the Americas today. The other ten are found in Africa, Asia, and Australia. The American crocodile, which reaches a maximum length of 16 feet (5 m), is only found in the United States in southern Florida. From there it ranges through the West Indies into Mexico and northern South America. Its population is vulnerable, meaning it is not yet endangered, but it will need to be protected.

Morelet's crocodile, found in Mexico and Central America, nearly went extinct, but conservation efforts have helped it recover, and it is now a species of least concern. It grows to 10 feet (3 m) in length.

The Cuban crocodile is critically endangered and is now found in only a few places in Cuba. Only a few thousand remain. The Orinoco crocodile, found only in northern South America, is also critically endangered. Once reaching lengths of up to 22 feet (6.6 m)—almost as much as the saltwater crocodile—it is now much smaller in size.

Other crocodilians have not fared as well as the saltwater crocodile. Of the fourteen species of true crocodiles living on Earth today, four are critically endangered. When a species is critically endangered, it is one step away from going extinct in the wild. Three other species of crocodile are not yet critically endangered, but are not far behind.

Lands Lost

Although the saltwater crocodile has made a comeback, it will need continued protection going forward. The major threat it faces today is habitat destruction. Wetlands, such as swamps, are drained to make way for farms, ranches, or human dwellings. When swamps are destroyed, saltwater crocodiles and many other species of animal lose their homes. When people build close to rivers, they are more likely to encounter crocodiles. The crocodiles are then killed or removed.

Forests are cleared for developments and to provide wood for lumber. Without forests, rainwater runs off the land, causing flooding and erosion, and carries dirt and pollutants into the waters of the saltwater crocodile's habitat.

Cutting down forests for development causes soil erosion, poor water quality, and climate change, and destroys the homes of many animals like the saltwater crocodile.

Human Hunters

Once saltwater crocodiles reach their full size, few animals will tackle them. At that size, their only natural enemy is people. They were once nearly exterminated by hunters who killed them for their skin. By the 1970s, most of the largest individuals were gone. Before that, saltwater crocodiles reached lengths of more than 27 feet (8 m), compared to a maximum of 23 feet (7 m) today.

Saltwater crocodiles, and sometimes their eggs, are now protected throughout most of their range, but that doesn't stop people from killing them. They are killed for their skin, for food, or simply because people are afraid of them. Some fishermen kill them so they don't have to compete with them for fish.

In some remote areas, such as Indonesia, it is hard to protect the saltwater crocodile because some people rely on it for food. Crocodile skins may also provide some people with their only source of income.

Unfortunately for the saltwater crocodile, it has the most valuable skin of any other crocodilian. All crocodilians have osteoderms along their back, but many also have them in the skin of their belly. Saltwater crocodiles do not. Because the osteoderms make it difficult to tan the hide into leather, dealers will pay more for the smooth belly skin of the saltwater crocodile. Illegal hunting still threatens the saltwater crocodile.

Saving the Saltie

Efforts to help the saltwater crocodile include creating laws, setting aside nature reserves, restocking, farming, education, and tourism. Laws against illegally hunting saltwater crocodiles now exist throughout their range, although they are not always enforced, especially in remote areas.

Kakadu National Park in northern Australia is home to thousands of saltwater crocodiles, living as they did millions of years ago.

Nature reserves such as national parks, where crocodiles can live in the wild without humans interfering in their habitat, have made a big difference. These reserves may be managed by a country's government, a private landowner, a charity, or a research organization. The purpose of a nature reserve is to protect the physical features of an area, such as its rivers and rock formations, as well as its plants and animals. Kakadu National Park, covering thousands of square miles, is a reserve in northern Australia that has allowed saltwater crocodiles to thrive naturally as they always have.

Crocodile Farms

Another conservation effort is the restocking programs that involve releasing young saltwater crocodiles back into natural habitats. The young for restocking may come from breeding programs on crocodile farms, or they may come from eggs collected in the wild and raised in captivity. Crocodile farms must obtain a permit to harvest only a certain number of eggs from the wild. Restocking programs in Australia and India have been very successful at returning saltwater crocodiles to the wild.

Some crocodile farms may also raise saltwater crocodiles to provide skins for the leather trade. Because saltwater crocodile leather is in such high demand, farming has become profitable. When saltwater crocodiles are raised for the leather trade, farmers use nest temperature to make sure that they produce mostly males. Because males grow faster than females, crocodile farmers can sell the skins sooner and make a larger profit.

Raising saltwater crocodiles in captivity for their leather has taken the pressure off of wild crocodile populations. Because farms can produce so many skins, hunters and poachers can no longer get the high prices they once demanded. Not everyone agrees with crocodile farming, however. Many are concerned about the welfare of the animals that are kept on the farms, and others feel crocodiles shouldn't be killed at all for their skins.

Croc Wise

Education has played a big part in helping to change peoples' attitudes about the saltwater crocodile. When people know more about an animal species, they are more likely to want to save it. Community awareness programs have helped by teaching people how to be safe when they are in saltwater crocodile habitats.

For example, new guidelines released in 2013 in Queensland, Australia, teach people how to avoid being attacked by a saltwater crocodile. They call it their "Croc Wise" program. The rules for staying safe include no swimming or wading in places where crocodiles may live. People who fish are warned to stay back from the water's edge, and to never clean fish or throw away fish scraps in or near the water.

Recreational boaters are reminded that it is illegal to come within 33 feet (10 m) of saltwater crocodiles in the wild, or to harass, feed, or interfere with them in any way. And, of course, they are told never to dangle their arms or legs over the side of a boat. The list goes on, but all of the Croc Wise rules are intended to protect both people and crocodiles.

Tourist Attraction

Crocodiles have always been a big draw at animal parks and zoos, but now people can take adventure tours to see them in the wild. The saltwater crocodile in its natural habitat then becomes economically valuable to people, which benefits conservation efforts, not only for the crocodile but also for all of the wildlife in the area.

Commercial boaters can apply for a special license to run tours in crocodile territories. Following strict safety rules, the license allows them to more closely approach the crocodiles for observation and photography. In some cases, tourists are thrilled when a naturalist dangles food from a pole out over the water to entice a gigantic saltwater crocodile to leap from the water after the treat.

For saltwater crocodiles to continue to prosper for another 200 million years, people will have to be willing to coexist with them. With saltwater crocodile populations increasing throughout the species' range, people have already come a long way toward accomplishing that goal. With their help, this fierce predator, skillful communicator, and protective parent will live on.

An 18-foot-long (5.5-meter) saltwater crocodile nicknamed Brutus thrills tourists by leaping from the water to grab a piece of meat.

GLOSSARY

alveoli - (*singular*, alveolus) the many tiny air sacs of the lungs where gas exchange takes place

aorta - the main artery leaving the heart that supplies oxygen-rich blood to the body

bronchi - (*singular*, bronchus) the air passages of the lungs that branch off from the trachea or windpipe

carcass - the dead body of an animal

carnivorous - meat eating or predatory

dominant - refers to an animal that has the highest rank in a social hierarchy and the greatest access to a territory, food, and mates

embryo - an unhatched or unborn offspring in the process of development

estuarine - relating to an estuary, or the mouth of a large river, where the salty ocean tide mixes with freshwater

excreted - expelled or eliminated as waste from the body

feral - in a wild state, especially after escaping from captivity or domestication

habitat - the natural environment of a plant or animal

hypotheses - possible explanations made on the basis of limited evidence that are used as a starting point for further study

mottled - marked with spots or smears of color

predator - an animal that hunts, kills, and eats other animals

prey - an animal that is hunted, killed, and eaten by another animal

primitive - belonging to, or seeming to come from, an early time in the very ancient past

riparian - relating to, or situated on, the banks of a river

scutes - thickened, bony plates on the back of a crocodile

shunt - a hole or small passage which allows liquids to be turned aside or moved to an alternative course

vertebrates - animals that possess a backbone or spinal column, including mammals, birds, reptiles, amphibians, and fish

FIND OUT MORE

Books
Alderton, David. *Crocodiles and Alligators of the World.* London, England: Blandford Publishing, 1991.

Cheatham, Karyn Follis. *The Crocodile.* San Diego, CA: Lucent Books, 2001.

Grigg, Gordon. *Crocodile: The Largest Reptile.* Collingwood, Australia: CSIRO Publishing, 2009.

Websites
Marine Bio
marinebio.org/species.asp?id=187
Explore the history of saltwater crocodiles, their habitat, and feeding behavior. Several exciting videos about crocodiles and other animals in the wild are also available.

National Geographic
animals.nationalgeographic.com/animals/reptiles/saltwater-crocodile
Discover more about the largest crocodilians on Earth. This website requires a free membership so please ask an adult for assistance with logging on.

Queensland Government Department of Environment and Heritage Protection
www.ehp.qld.gov.au/wildlife/livingwith/crocodiles/estuarine_crocodile.html
Learn about the lives of estuarine crocodiles and view several photos of them in various habitats.

INDEX

Page numbers in **boldface** are illustrations.

alveoli, 21–22
aorta, 22

bronchi, 21–22

carcass, 18
carnivorous, 8, 15

dominant, 26

embryo, 29
estuarine, 10, 11
excreted, 21

feral, 30

habitat, 9, 38, 40, 41–42
hypotheses, 6

mottled, 17

predator, 5, 11, 15, 30, 32, 35, 42
prey, 5, 15, **16**, **17**, 18
primitive, 15, 26

riparian, 11

saltwater crocodiles
    food preferences, 15–18
    mating, 28–29
    physical characteristics, 5, 17–22
scutes, 6, **18**, 19
shunt, 22

vertebrates, 15

ABOUT THE AUTHOR

Susan Schafer is an author, artist, and educator with a passion for animals. She has written numerous books about animals, including horses, turkey vultures, tigers, the Komodo dragon, and the Galapagos tortoise. The latter was selected as an Outstanding Science Trade Book for Children by the National Science Teachers Association. Schafer has spent many years working in the field of zoology, including at the world-famous San Diego Zoo and the Taronga Park Zoo in Sydney, Australia. She has traveled the world, studying the animals she loves in their natural environments. To learn more about Schafer and the animal art she has created from her many memories, visit www.susanfschaferstudio.com.